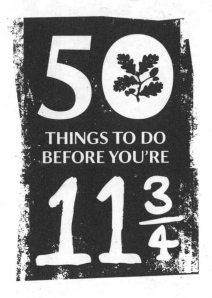

50

THINGS TO DO BEFORE YOU'RE

11 ¾

National Trust

50

THINGS TO DO
BEFORE YOU'RE

11 ¾

My adventure notebook
for wild times outdoors

National Trust

First published in the United Kingdom in 2013 by
National Trust Books
10 Southcombe Street, London W14 0RA

An imprint of Anova Books Company Ltd

© National Trust 2013
The National Trust is a registered charity, no. 205846

Based on original designs for the National Trust by 18 feet and rising

Produced by SP Creative Design
Photographs ©National Trust Images/Josh Cole; p.75 National Trust
Images/John Millar
Illustrations by N. Duncan Mills

ISBN: 9781907892677

A CIP catalogue record for this book is available from
the British Library.

Printed and bound by Lego S.p.A., Italy

This book can be ordered direct from the publisher at
the website www.anovabooks com, or try your local
bookshop. Also available at National Trust shops and
www.nationaltrust.org.uk/shop

Contents

Adventurer

Discoverer

Ranger

Tracker

Explorer

50 things to do before you're 11¾

Welcome to the great outdoors...
Crazy creatures, awesome antics, hidden
treasures! Thrills, hills, sun and fun, there's
everything you need for an excellent adventure!
With help from kids all over the country,
we've put together a list of great
challenges for you; the ultimate
50 things to do before you're
11¾, and we're making it as easy
as mud pie to do them somewhere
near you with a little helping hand
from the National Trust.

Caution: Some of them may cause extreme excitement.

Note to grown-ups: Children matter to the National Trust, so we recommend that all these activities are supervised by an adult. We trust that you will make your own judgement about what is safe and suitable for the ability of your child. Just remember to have fun!

Where do I begin?

Your adventure notebook will take you into the woods and onto the water, up huge hills and down to the beach. Plus there are plenty of ways to make the most of what's closer to home. At the National Trust we have all the space you'll need; we don't mind if you make some noise or get mucky, so long as you always have a grown-up with you to make sure you're still in one piece by the time you're 11¾.

This book consists of 5 sections of 10 activities, each getting more adventurous as you go through.

At our 50 things website, you'll be able to design your very own virtual explorer. You and your family will get advice and guidance about how to complete your 50 things. You can also find out which of our places are near you and which of the 50 things you can do there. Sign up online to tick off your adventures, upload pictures and explore the 50 things in more detail. You'll also find lots of hints and tips on how to become a 50 things expert safely.

Continue the adventure online

nationaltrust.org.uk/50things

Register for free on our website and you'll unlock a cheeky explorer friend who'll guide you through the 50 things. The more adventures you take, the more rewards you'll unlock.

Keep this a secret, but if you log all 50 things online you'll earn your National Trust Explorer Medal which holds special powers, only revealed to those brave enough to complete everything before they turn 11¾.

'Mum and Dad took me and my brother to Clumber Park in Worksop to meet my cousins and we did this. It was great fun'

Recommended by Oliver, aged 6

Adventurer

Tick off each activity as you complete it.

1. Climb a tree ☐
2. Roll down a really big hill ☐
3. Camp out in the wild ☐
4. Build a den ☐
5. Skim a stone ☐
6. Run around in the rain ☐
7. Fly a kite ☐
8. Catch a fish with a net ☐
9. Eat an apple from a tree ☐
10. Play conkers ☐

1. Climb a tree

Check out the view!

What you need:

- A tree with big strong branches you can reach from the ground
- Trainers or boots - you don't want splinters in your toes
- A big wave for everyone down below

See if you can collect some leaves on the way down and stick one on this page:

TOP TIP

Keep three of your arms and legs on the tree at all times, and always be sure to never forget to check it's dry before you climb.

Find out what kind of tree you climbed and write it here:

Date completed: Day _____ Month _____ Year _____

2. Roll down a really big hill

It's the fun way to get to the bottom.

What you need:

- A grassy hill
- A clear run with nothing you might bump into

Rolling down the hill makes you feel all dizzy and swirly. Can you draw an impression of yourself here after you've finished rolling?

TOP TIP

A fun roll is a fast roll. To really pick up speed lie on the grass, make your body into the shape of a sausage and roll down the hill sideways. Watch out for poo from animals like sheep, as it can spread nasty germs.

How many times did you roll over? Write it here:

Date completed: Day _____ Month _____ Year _____

3. Camp out in the wild

Why sleep in a boring bed when you can sleep outside like a cowboy?

What you need:

– Go back to basics with a tent, ground mat and sleeping bag...or you can make yourself really cosy by taking your favourite pillow, duvet and a blow-up mattress

– Everyone needs a torch when they're camping out

What nature sounds did you hear in the night?

Can you draw a picture of one of the animals that you heard?

TOP TIP

Before setting up your tent, pick a nice flat open area and clear away any stones or branches that might wake you up if you roll on them.

Keep an eye out for bats, moths and owls which only come out at night

Date completed: Day _____ Month _____ Year _____

4. Build a den

Branches, twigs and leaves make surprisingly cosy dens.

What you need:

- Branches, twigs, leaves and mud, all of which are generously provided by nature for free
- Leave the power tools at home, you won't need them here

Make a list of all the things you found outside to use as building materials. Take a photo of you in your den and stick it here:

> **TOP TIP**
>
> Choose a dry flat spot for the most solid den and never build with sharp objects. It could help to start by leaning sticks against a low tree branch like a wig-wam.

Date completed: Day _____ Month _____ Year _____

5. Skim a stone

Can you do four bounces?

What you need:

- Flat water, like a pond, lake or the sea on a calm day
- Somewhere to stand where you won't fall in when you throw really hard
- Some flat stones from near the water's edge

Not all water ripples are made from skimming stones. Sometimes they are made from things under the water. Can you draw something else you've seen that makes water ripple?

TOP TIP

Choose your stone carefully: the smoother, rounder and flatter the better. Throw it hard and low so it spins quickly across the top of the water. Make sure there's nothing in the water you might hit, like ducks or swimmers!

How many bounces did your stone make? Write it here:

Date completed: Day _____ Month _____ Year _____

18

6. Run around in the rain

Time to make a splash!

What you need:

- A rainy day
- Welly boots
- A raincoat
- Or a towel and a change of clothes

Some animals love getting wet. Make a list of animals you think are happy when it rains and draw a picture of your favourite one here:

Date completed: Day _____ Month _____ Year _____

7. Fly a kite

A windy day is a perfect day for flying a kite.

What you need:

- Plenty of wind
- A wide open space
- A kite!

Can you design a colourful pattern on the kite below?

Date completed: Day _____ Month _____ Year _____

8. Catch a fish with a net

You have to be quick to catch a fish!

What you need:

- Somewhere fish live (the sea, a river, a canal or a lake)
- Somewhere you can stand or sit for a while safely
- A net
- Permission from the person who owns the land

Draw a picture of your fish and give it a name.

TOP TIP

Fishing takes time and patience: find someone who knows all about fishing to help you catch a whopper. Don't forget that fish like where they live and want to stay there. Always put them quickly and carefully back into the water. For more help and advice visit the 50 things website.

Look carefully to see if you've caught any little fish such as sticklebacks and minnows which are found in streams

What fish did you catch?

Date completed: Day _____ Month _____ Year _____

9. Eat an apple straight from a tree

Money doesn't grow on trees but apples do!

What you need:

- An apple tree – with eating apples
- Somebody to help you reach the branches
- Permission from whoever owns the tree

There are more than 700 different types of apples in the UK. What is the name of the one you picked and what colour was it?

TOP TIP

The ripest apples are on the outside branches of the tree, furthest away from the trunk. Don't eat raw cooking apples – they could give you a bad tummy ache.

Nibbles the caterpillar lives in this apple.

See if you can turn it into a nice cosy home for him:

Date completed: Day _____ Month _____ Year _____

10. Play conkers

It's not always the biggest conker that wins!

What you need:

- A conker
- Some string
- A worthy opponent
- A grown-up to help you get the string through the conker

In the template below, can you design some war paint for your conker to go into battle with? Why not try painting it onto your real conker, Give it a name and write it here: too?

TOP TIP

To choose a killer conker, put some conkers in a bucket of water; all those that sink to the bottom are winners, those that float are losers. Ask your Mum or Dad to teach you how to play. If they can't remember (it's a while since they were kids!) you can check out the details on the 50 things website.

Date completed: Day _____ Month _____ Year _____

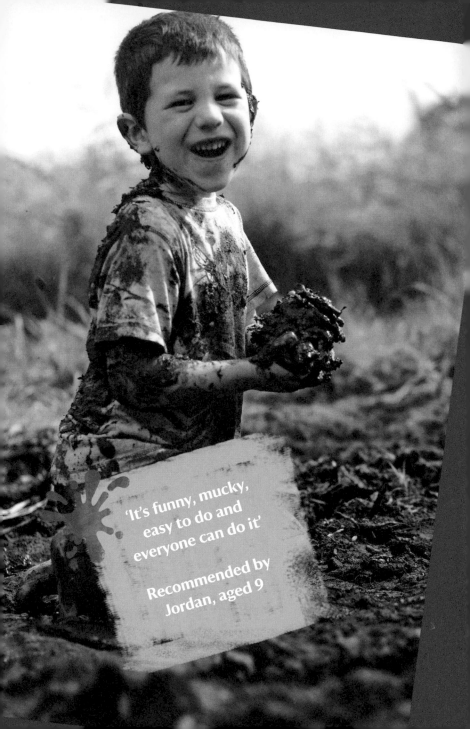

'It's funny, mucky, easy to do and everyone can do it'

Recommended by Jordan, aged 9

50. Canoe down a river

See the world from a duck's point of view.

What you need:

- A canoe
- Paddles
- A life jacket
- A river
- Expert advice and supervision

Did you see any wildlife when you were canoeing?

TOP TIP

Going round and round in circles can get a bit boring. Paddle evenly on both sides to go in a straight line and actually get somewhere. This isn't the kind of thing you do everyday – join a class or go to an event. Visit the 50 things website to find out more.

Draw what you saw in the space below:

Look out for dragonflies and water birds, like herons and moorhens. You might even spot a little egret too!

Date completed: Day _____ Month _____ Year _____

Discoverer

Tick off each activity as you complete it.

11. Go on a really long bike ride ☐

12. Make a trail with sticks ☐

13. Make a mud pie ☐

14. Dam a stream ☐

15. Play in the snow ☐

16. Make a daisy chain ☐

17. Set up a snail race ☐

18. Create some wild art ☐

19. Play pooh sticks ☐

20. Jump over waves ☐

11. Go on a really long bike ride

The speedy way to explore the great outdoors.

What you need:

- A bike which is in good working order
- A bike helmet
- A grown-up to accompany you on your biking adventure

TOP TIP

Take a map with you, so you know where you're going!

Draw a map of your bike ride below so you can show your friends exactly where you went:

Date completed: Day _____ Month _____ Year _____

12. Make a trail with sticks

Use sticks as arrows and mark a path through the woods.

What you need:

- Lots of straight sticks to lay on the ground in the shape of arrows so they're really clear for your friends and family to follow

Draw or stick a picture of you all at the end of your trail here:

TOP TIP

You can make the trail really good fun by going over logs and around trees, and bring something fun to hide as a treasure at the end of it.

How many sticks did you use to make your trail? Write it here:

Date completed: Day _____ Month _____ Year _____

13. Make a mud pie

Recipe: Mud. More mud.

What you need:

- Lots of mud
- Stones and leaves for decorating your pie
- Optional extras include bucket, spade, water and sticks to help you move the mud around

Oozy sticky mud makes great finger prints. Can you and your friends or family all make a thumbprint in the space below to remember your day? You could even turn them into little thumb people.

TOP TIP

Mud pies might look delicious but they don't taste great, so never eat a mud pie. Don't forget to wash your hands afterwards.

Worms and lots of tiny animals actually live in mud, look out for them!

Date completed: Day _____ Month _____ Year _____

14. Dam a stream

It won't be long before the stream's a pond!

What you need:

– Twigs

– Branches

– Stones

– Rocks

What kind of animals do you think live near the river bank? Draw them here:

TOP TIP

What goes up must come down – you can have fun smashing down the dam once you've made it but don't go in too deep.

Date completed: Day _____ Month _____ Year _____

15. Play in the snow

Keep your fingers cosy and your toes toasty.

What you need:

– Lots of clean white snow
– Waterproof clothes and layers to keep you warm and dry

Ask someone to take a photo of you and your snow creation and stick it below:

TOP TIP

If you've made a snowman before then why not try making a snow sculpture of your favourite animal?

Give it a name and write it here:

Date completed: Day _____ Month _____ Year _____

16. Make a daisy chain

A perfect gift for the fairies.

What you need:

– Daisies

You can stick your daisy chain here when it's done or just one daisy if you have a long chain:

TOP TIP

Try to find daisies with long, thick stems to use to make the chain. They will be easier to make holes in and they won't break easily.

How many daisies did you use to make your chain?

Daisies don't really mind being picked as it makes them grow more flowers

Date completed: Day _____ Month _____ Year _____

17. Set up a snail race

On your marks, get set, go...slowly!

What you need:

- Some snails
- A circle of chalk to mark your finish line
- Team colours for your snails (stickers work well)

A snail's shell is its home and helps protect it from harm. Draw a picture of its spiralled shape and markings:

Write the name of the snail that came 1st here:

Date completed: Day _____ Month _____ Year _____

18. Create some wild art

What you need:

- A collection of leaves, twigs, feathers and seed pods
- Some paper, some glue
- A flat, dry surface to work on in a sheltered spot

Your picture or sculpture will likely be too big to include here, but you can take a photo of it and stick it in here or make a smaller picture with leftover leaves and feathers:

TOP TIP

Try to find materials that vary in colour and texture so you have lots of choice and can make something really interesting and individual.

Date completed: Day _____ Month _____ Year _____

19. Play pooh sticks

Get your sticks at the ready!

What you need:

- A good-sized stick and one you'll recognise (so you'll know who won!)
- A bridge with nicely flowing water running under it. But you must be careful of traffic if the bridge you're standing on is also a road

Which sticks, big, small, thick or thin won the most?

TOP TIP

Why not decorate your stick by tying a leaf or some grass to it so you know exactly which one is yours when it comes out from the other side of the bridge?

Write who came in 1st, 2nd and 3rd place here:

1st:

2nd:

3rd:

Date completed: Day _____ Month _____ Year _____

34

20. Jump over waves

Big, small, blue or green, all waves are great to jump over!

What you need:

- A spot where you know the depth of water you are entering before you start to make sure you don't go in too deep
- A grown-up to jump with you

What other animals can you think of that would be good at jumping over waves? Can you draw one of them jumping over the waves below?

TOP TIP

Watch out for underwater rocks or crevices which might hurt you, when picking your jumping spot.

Date completed: Day _____ Month _____ Year _____

'Climbing a hill is a good thing to do to keep you fit and the views you get when you are at the top are amazing'

Recommended by
Katy, aged 9

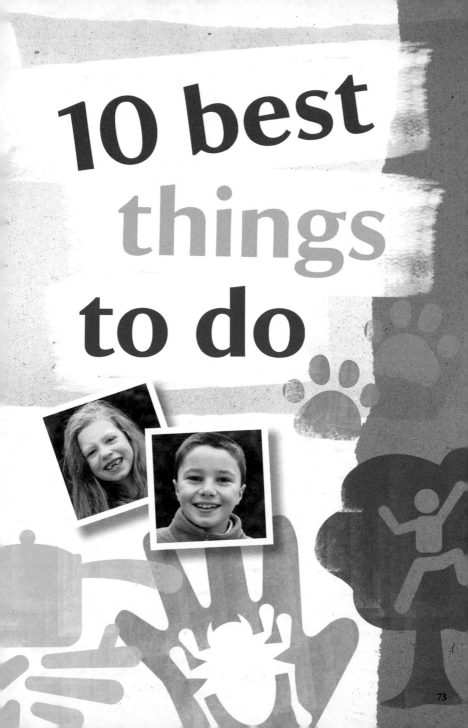

10 best things to do

1

Climb a tree (page 14)

Recommended by Jessica Swales,
aged 8, from North Yorkshire

Build a den (page 17)

Recommended by Mia McDade,
aged 7, from Cheshire

DID YOU KNOW?

As your old den rots, it
will be eaten away by
fungi, insects and other
invertebrates – all of which
love rotting wood.

2

3

Go on a really long bike ride (page 26)

Recommended by
Harry Wilson,
aged 10, from Bristol

DID YOU KNOW?

On a bicycle you can travel three times faster than you can walk for the same amount of energy.

Go on a walk
barefoot (page 41)

Recommended by Francesca
Carrannante, aged 8 from London

DID YOU KNOW?

There are 700 different
types of soil in England
and Wales alone.

4

5

Hunt for fossils and bones (page 43)

Recommended by
Kai Bickley, aged 6,
from the West Midlands

DID YOU KNOW?

The best time to
hunt for fossils is
just after a storm
when the waves have
uncovered new finds.

6

Hold a scary beast (page 47)

Recommended by Iona Howells, aged 11, from Kent

DID YOU KNOW?

There are over 40,000 different types of invertebrates in the UK, including more than 23,000 insects. Only a few of them bite or sting, though, such as ants and wasps.

7

Track wild animals (page 53)

Recommended by Sophia Tarling, aged 8, from Norfolk

Discover what's in a pond (page 54)

Recommended by Max Hodgson, aged 8, from the West Midlands

8

9

Go bird watching (page 65)

Recommended by Leif Wilson-Palmer, aged 8,
from Gloucestershire

DID YOU KNOW?

More than 600 species
of birds have been seen
in the UK.

10

Cook on a campfire

(page 68)

Recommended by
Kit Le Froy, aged 8,
from Cornwall

50 best places

 1. Climb a tree

Wallington
Northumberland

 2. Roll down a really big hill

Croome
Worcestershire

3. Camp out in the wild

Gibside
Tyne & Wear

 4. Build a den

Lyme Park, House and Garden
Cheshire

 5. Skim a stone

Fell Foot Park
Cumbria

6. Run around in the rain

Finch Foundry
Devon

 7. Fly a kite

Dunstable Downs
Bedfordshire

 8. Catch a fish with a net

Parke
Devon

 9. Eat an apple straight from a tree

Llanerchaeron
Ceredigion

 10. Play conkers

Osterley Park and House
London

 11. Go on a really long bike ride

Wimpole Estate
Cambridgeshire

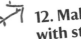 **12. Make a trail with sticks**

Longshaw and Eastern Moors
Derbyshire

13. Make a mud pie
Moseley Old Hall
Staffordshire

14. Dam a stream
Prior Park Landscape Garden
Somerset

15. Play in the snow
Bodiam Castle
Sussex

16. Make a daisy chain
Lacock Abbey
Wiltshire

17. Set up a snail race
Lyveden New Bield
Northamptonshire

18. Create some wild art
Sheringham Park
Norfolk

19. Play pooh sticks
Mottisfont
Hampshire

20. Jump over waves
Compton Bay and Downs
Isle of Wight

21. Pick blackberries growing in the wild
Castle Ward
County Down

22. Explore inside a tree
Hatfield Forest
Hertfordshire

23. Visit a farm
Cuckmere Valley
Sussex

24. Go on a walk barefoot

Strumble Head to Cardigan
Pembrokeshire

31. Hunt for bugs

Hardcastle Crags
Yorkshire

25. Make a grass trumpet

Hare Hill
Cheshire

32. Find some frogspawn

Springhill
County Londonderry

33. Catch a falling leaf

Rowallane Garden
County Down

26. Hunt for fossils and bones

Birling Gap and the Seven Sisters
Sussex

34. Track wild animals

Castle Drogo
Devon

27. Go star gazing

Tyntesfield
Somerset

35. Discover what's in a pond

Florence Court
County Fermanagh

28. Climb a huge hill

Ashridge Estate
Hertfordshire

36. Make a home for a wild animal

Fountains Abbey and Studley Royal
Yorkshire

29. Explore a cave

Yorkshire Dales: Upper Wharfedale
Yorkshire

30. Hold a scary beast

Clumber Park
Nottinghamshire

43. Build a raft

Borrowdale
Cumbria

44. Go bird watching

Kingston Lacy
Dorset

37. Check out the crazy creatures in a rock pool

South Milton Sands
Devon

45. Find your way with a map and compass

Chartwell
Kent

38. Bring up a butterfly

Anglesey Abbey,
Cambridgeshire

46. Try rock climbing

Brimham Rocks
Yorkshire

39. Catch a crab

Plas Newydd
Gwynedd

47. Cook on a campfire

Stackpole
Pembrokeshire

40. Go on a nature walk at night

Nostell Priory
Yorkshire

48. Learn to ride a horse

Clandon Park
Surrey

41. Plant it, grow it, eat it

Tredegar House
Newport

49. Find a geocache

Sizergh
Cumbria

42. Go swimming in the sea

Llŷn Peninsula
Gwynedd

50. Canoe down a river

Brancaster Millennium Activity Centre
Norfolk

Spring

32. Find some frogspawn

It's amazing finding frogs' eggs in a pond and to think they will grow into tadpoles and then into frogs!

Recommended by Leon, aged 5, East Sussex

44. Go bird watching

Birds are amazing animals and you might spot really rare ones

Recommended by Olivia, aged 9, Yorkshire

28. Climb a huge hill

❛ Because everyone can do it if they try. Climbing a hill is a good thing to do to keep you fit and the views you get when you are at the top are amazing! ❜

Recommended by Katy, aged 9, Staffordshire

31. Hunt for bugs

❛ Some people are scared of creepy crawlies but they mean us no harm ❜

Recommended by Natalie, aged 11, Midlothian

41. Plant it, grow it, eat it

❛ I really like gardening and growing, you have fun getting mucky ❜

Recommended by Katie, aged 10, Hampshire

Summer

3. Camp out in the wild

It will let you hear what happens at night out in nature!

Recommended by Lily, aged 8, West Sussex

38. Bring up a butterfly

It's really adventurous and gives you a chance to discover the life of a butterfly

Recommended by Chloe, aged 11, Northumberland

2. Roll down a really big hill

It is the BEST fun and I have done it with so many friends and we have all loved it

Recommended by LouLou, aged 11, Lincolnshire

39. Catch a crab

It's a really fun thing to do at the beach. You could have medals for the winners, gold is the one with the biggest crab. Remember to put the crabs back in the sea afterwards

Recommended by Olivia, aged 9, Devon

42. Go swimming in the sea

It isn't hard to do and it's different to swimming in a swimming pool

Recommended by Eloise, aged 9, Essex

14. Dam a stream

It is fun to work out where the water is getting through and find ways to block it off

Recommended by Alice, aged 8, Oxfordshire

46. Try rock climbing

Rock climbing should be included because it's fabulous

Recommended by Lucy, aged 10, Merseyside

9. Eat an apple straight from a tree

I have an orchard in my front garden and this is one of my most favourite things to do

Recommended by Kevin, aged 5, County Down

30. Hold a scary beast

It gives you a chance to hold it and not be frightened

Recommended by Lucy, aged 10, Somerset

49. Find a geocache

It turns a walk into an adventure and you have to watch out for muggles (who are not geocachers) so it is secret. I have to work out puzzles and write down what I have found, and adults enjoy it too

Recommended by James, aged 5, Yorkshire

21. Pick blackberries growing in the wild

"Because blackberries are tasty and easy to find, and it is fun cooking with them"

Recommended by Zoë, aged 9, Staffordshire

40. Go on a nature walk at night

"I did it when it was my 4th birthday with my Mum, Dad and brother. We walked in some fields and found a badger track, saw some rabbits and looked for the moon. The best bits were seeing the bats flying and looking at the stars."

Recommended by Ned, aged 4, Gloucestershire

10. Play conkers

"Because it's a fun game you can enjoy, and you can decorate your conkers, too"

Recommended by Tiana, aged 11, Surrey

12. Make a trail with sticks

"I did this with my Mummy, Daddy and brother and it was really fun using sticks as arrows to show the way"

Recommended by Joshua, aged 8, London

Winter

34. Track wild animals

"You can go for long walks in woods or forests looking for animal tracks to follow and hopefully see animals close up"

Recommended by Daniel, aged 6, London

22. Explore inside a tree

"Looking inside a tree is fun. I climbed inside and hid from my Mum. Inside one of the trees the pattern looked like a face. It was a bit scary. I laughed when my Mum found me. I had a magnifying glass so I could look for mini beasts. The trees were really old"

Recommended by Wilf, aged 5, Gloucestershire

15. Play in the snow

"It's magical"

Recommended by Lily, aged 8, West Sussex

27. Go star gazing

When I was camping me and my Mum were looking at the stars and I saw the Plough and Orion's Belt. I have asked for an astronomy book for my birthday so that I can look for more. I think other children would like it too

Recommended by Amy, aged 9, Oxfordshire

45. Find your way with a map and compass

It is a really fun activity and adults can join in too

Recommended by Ben, aged 11, Cleveland

26. Hunt for fossils and bones

It's fun going on a walk and looking for fossils and very exciting if you find one

Recommended by Rebecca, aged 11, Shropshire

Tracker

Tick off each activity as you complete it.

31. Hunt for bugs ☐

32. Find some frogspawn ☐

33. Catch a falling leaf ☐

34. Track wild animals ☐

35. Discover what's in a pond ☐

36. Make a home for a
    wild animal ☐

37. Check out the crazy
    creatures in a rock pool ☐

38. Bring up a butterfly ☐

39. Catch a crab ☐

40. Go on a nature walk
    at night ☐

31. Hunt for bugs

What's the creepiest crawly you can find?

What you need:

- Places where bugs like to hide, such as under rocks, in the mud or the bark of fallen trees

Draw the best bug you found:

If your bug could talk, what would it say to you?

Date completed: Day _____ Month _____ Year _____

32. Find some frogspawn

**You think frogspawn looks weird?
Just wait until they become tadpoles!**

What you need:

- A bucket or a plastic tub
- A net to scoop them out
- A grown-up to supervise while you scoop
- Somewhere you can stand or sit safely

Can you draw what you think the frogspawn might look like when it's halfway to being a frog? You'll have to go back in a few weeks to see if you're right!

TOP TIP

Spring is the best time to find frogspawn but don't take the frogspawn away – they're happy in their home. Once you've had a look, put them back in the pond.

A frog can lay around 5,000 eggs at once that can take over a month to turn to tadpoles!

Date completed: Day _____ Month _____ Year _____

33. Catch a falling leaf

It's harder than you think.

What you need:

– A tree with lots of big leaves

Stick your favourite leaf on this page.

Why is this your favourite?

TOP TIP

Leaves start to fall off trees in autumn, so it's the best time of year to try catching them. If it's a windy day, stand so the wind blows into you – it will help bring the leaves towards you.

What type of tree does the leaf come from?

Date completed: Day _____ Month _____ Year _____

34. Track wild animals

Animals are easy to find if you follow their footprints, eathers, fur and poo.

What you need:

- Sharp eyes
- Trainers or boots so you can track down animals wherever they roam

Draw a picture of the footprints you find on this page.

What animal do you think they come from?

TOP TIP

Remember, animals don't wear shoes so their footprints don't all look the same. From a horse's hoof to a rabbit's paw, learn what you're looking for. Whatever you do, don't touch the poo!

How many tracks did you come across? Write the number here:

Date completed: Day _____ Month _____ Year _____

35. Discover what's in a pond

Murky pond water is full of life. Scoop some out into a tub and check out what lurks beneath.

What you need:

- A clean, empty plastic tub
- A fine net
- Somewhere you can stand or sit safely
- A grown-up to go with you

Draw what you found at the bottom of your net:

TOP TIP

Scoop the net 3 times in a figure-of-eight to pick up the littlest creatures and empty the contents into the tub. If you don't spot anything at first, take a closer look. Pond life tends to be quite tiny. Remember to return the mini-beasts to their homes.

Date completed: Day _____ Month _____ Year _____

36. Make a home for a wild animal

It's not just dogs, cats, hamsters and fish that need homes.

What you need:

- Bits and pieces that you will have in the garden, such as moss, twigs or stones
- String or glue to help fasten it all together
- A flat, dry and sheltered surface to work on

What kind of animals moved into your home?

How long did they stay for?

TOP TIP

All sorts of animals need homes. You could try making a bug hotel, hedgehog house or even a bird box. Once it's completed, think about the best place to put it. Some animals prefer sunshine while others like shade.

Date completed: Day _____ Month _____ Year _____

37. Check out the crazy creatures in a rock pool

What's the weirdest looking thing you can find?

What you need:

- A clean plastic tub or bucket to scoop the water out
- A small net to help you catch things
- A low tide

What's the weirdest thing you found in the rock pool?

Can you draw it here?

TOP TIP

Keep your hands out of the pool or you might feel a little nibble or pinch! These crazy creatures like where they live, so don't forget to put them back afterwards.

Starfish can push their stomachs out of their mouths so they can gobble up and digest anything that's too big to swallow!

Date completed: Day _____ Month _____ Year _____

38. Bring up a butterfly

Once a caterpillar makes its chrysalis, it may become a beautiful butterfly in less than six weeks.

What you need:

- A caterpillar
- A large plastic tub with small holes in the lid
- Leaves from one of the caterpillar's favourite plants
- Slightly damp soil or sand to line the bottom of the tub
- A twig or two to lean against the side of the tub

Draw a picture of how your caterpillar looks each week so you can show how it's changed:

Week 1

Week 2

Week 3

Week 4

Week 5

Week 6

Date completed: Day _____ Month _____ Year _____

39. Catch a crab

With the right bait and a piece of string it's easier than you might think.

What you need:

- String or crab line
- A good spot by the sea to get settled
- Scraps of bacon or fish for the bait
- A bucket of water if you'd like to take a closer look before they go back in

Count up all the legs and claws on the crab you catch and make a sketch of what it looks like:

TOP TIP

Tie the stone and bait to the end of the string so it sinks properly. When you feel it tugging, pull the string up at a good pace – too fast and the crab will fall off, too slowly and it will eat all the bait. Be careful when picking up crabs (they're not afraid to use those pincers) and put them back in the water afterwards.

Date completed: Day _____ Month _____ Year _____

40. Go on a nature walk at night

Some creatures only come out at night so this is the only chance you've got of spotting them!

What you need:

- A torch
- A grown-up who can show you where to look
- Trainers or boots – leave your slippers at home!
- Warm clothing (pyjamas don't count!)

Switch off your torch and stand silently for 5 minutes to fully experience how life is for animals in the dark.

Write what you heard below:

TOP TIP

Only use your torch when you really need to. These animals aren't afraid of the dark. They are afraid of noisy humans though, so be as quiet as a mouse.

Date completed: Day _____ Month _____ Year _____

'Cooking on a campfire is an essential survival skill everyone should learn and is a cool thing to end a wild adventure in the woods with'

Recommended by Matthew, aged 11

Explorer

Tick off each activity as you complete it.

41. Plant it, grow it, eat it ☐

42. Go swimming in the sea ☐

43. Build a raft ☐

44. Go bird watching ☐

45. Find your way with a map and compass ☐

46. Try rock climbing ☐

47. Cook on a campfire ☐

48. Learn to ride a horse ☐

49. Find a geocache ☐

50. Canoe down a river ☐

Date completed: Day _____ Month _____ Year _____

41. Plant it, grow it, eat it

Just like you, fruit and vegetables need a bit of time to grow but they're definitely worth the wait.

What you need:

- Fruit or vegetable plants or seeds
- A pot to plant them in
- Peat-free compost

Can you draw a picture of your plant each week to show how it grows?

TOP TIP

Make sure you plant the right thing at the right time. Visit www.eatseasonably.co.uk for all the information you need to grow your own.

Home-grown food tastes best! Try growing different fruit or vegetables across the year and see if you agree

Date completed: Day _____ Month _____ Year _____

42. Go swimming in the sea

It's much more fun than swimming in a pool.

What you need:

– Choose a warm, sunny day
– Goggles
– An adult to swim with you
– A towel to dry-off after your swim

When you dry off from your swim, sit on the beach and look out to sea. What can you spot on the horizon?

TOP TIP

The sea can be powerful. With a grown-up, look for an area where the water is calm and not too deep.

Draw what you see in the binoculars below:

Date completed: Day _____ Month _____ Year _____

43. Build a raft

It's a pirate's life for me, just watch out for the ducks!

What you need:

- Sticks and string to tie them all together
- A pond or small stream to test your raft
- Shoes that don't matter if they get wet
- A grown-up to help you near the water

Draw a diagram of your raft below and see if your friends can follow your instructions to build their own rafts too:

TOP TIP

When launching a raft look for some calm water which isn't too deep to give the raft the best chance of launching, not sinking! If you're adventurous, join a class or event where you can build a raft big enough for you to race on.

Date completed: Day _____ Month _____ Year _____

44. Go bird watching

Keep silent as a mouse and watch the birds at play.

What you need:

- A place where birds like to fly or search for food
- A quiet spot to sit and hide while you watch the birds
- A pair of binoculars and a camera

Why not make a list of all the birds you spot so that you can compare it with other adventurers?

Draw a picture or stick a photo of a bird you spot here:

TOP TIP

Birds get frightened off very easily – stay quiet so they don't fly away before you can identify them.

Nearly 600 different types of birds have been seen in the UK!

Date completed: Day _____ Month _____ Year _____

45. Find your way with a map and compass

You'll never get lost if you can use these trusty tools.

What you need:

- A map
- A compass
- A destination
- A whistle to let people know where you are

Draw your own map of where you went:

TOP TIP

Always work out where you are on the map before you even set off so you know you're starting in the right place. It also helps if you hold the map the right way round!

Date completed: Day _____ Month _____ Year _____

46. Try rock climbing

Keep your eyes peeled for some big cracks and places to get a good grip.

What you need:

- A rock that's stable and isn't wet or too steep
- Trainers for grip
- An expert to help you, as even professional rock climbers never climb alone

Stick a photo of you rock climbing here:

TOP TIP

Rocks can be slippery, especially if wet. Build up slowly before venturing too high and soon you'll be climbing Bond-style. This isn't the kind of thing you do everyday, so join a class or go to an event. Visit the 50 things website to find out more.

How many metres do you think you climbed overall? Write it here so you can try and beat it next time round.

Date completed: Day _____ Month _____ Year _____

47. Cook on a campfire

There's no kitchen in the great outdoors but you don't have to miss dinner.

What you need:

- A campfire
- Your chosen ingredients
- Cooking equipment, such as skewers for your marshmallows, a pot for your beans or a pan for your bangers
- A grown-up to check you don't spoil dinner

Write a recipe for something that you cooked on the campfire:

TOP TIP

This is not the time for a Sunday roast with all the trimmings. Keep it simple at first with food that cooks quickly and easily. Sausages, soups or beans all work well.

Date completed: Day _____ Month _____ Year _____

48. Learn to ride a horse

Learn to ride a horse like a proper cowboy.

What you need:

- An activity centre or stables where you can ride
- A grown-up to instruct you
- A riding hat, comfortable (but not baggy) clothes and boots or trainers

Stick a photo of you riding a horse here:

TOP TIP

Remember to listen very carefully to your instructor, so that you can learn to ride your horse safely.

What would your horse's racing name be? Write it here:

Date completed: Day _____ Month _____ Year _____

49. Find a geocache

With over a million in the world, there must be one around here somewhere…

What you need:

– A smartphone or handheld GPS

Draw what was inside your geocache:

TOP TIP

Get involved and join a geocache community online. The largest is www.geocaching.com

What would you leave inside a geocache for someone else to find? Write a list in this box:

Date completed: Day _____ Month _____•_____ Year _____

Ranger

Tick off each activity as you complete it.

21. Pick blackberries growing in the wild ☐

22. Explore inside a tree ☐

23. Visit a farm ☐

24. Go on a walk barefoot ☐

25. Make a grass trumpet ☐

26. Hunt for fossils and bones ☐

27. Go star gazing ☐

28. Climb a huge hill ☐

29. Explore a cave ☐

30. Hold a scary beast ☐

21. Pick blackberries growing in the wild

They're not just tasty treats, they make great drawing tools too.

What you need:

- Bushes full of blackberries
- A stick to lift branches while you pick to avoid getting spiked by thorns
- Help from a grown-up who knows what they're doing

Can you draw a picture with your fingers just using blackberry juice?

TOP TIP

September is a prime time to pick blackberries from hedgerows – they're everywhere! Remember to wash your blackberries before eating as they've been out in the wild and don't forget to leave some for the birds!

Date completed: Day _____ Month _____ Year _____

22. Explore inside a tree

Some trees have hollows so big you can climb right inside.

What you need:

– A tree with a big hole in it
– A magnifying glass to look for mini-beasts
– A torch to look deep into the holes

Use some coloured crayons to take a rubbing of the tree that you climbed into. Stick it in here:

TOP TIP

The oldest trees have the biggest hollows, so look for the big tall trees.

Lots of insects live inside hollow trees, like beetles, eating the rotting wood. Look closely and you'll see their burrowing holes

Date completed: Day _____ Month _____ Year _____

23. Visit a farm

One of the best places to get up close and personal with new furry friends.

What you need:

- A farm you can visit with experts who can tell you all about the animals

Draw a picture of your favourite animal and write down what you learnt about it today:

TOP TIP

Make sure that after your farm visit, you wash your hands really well before you eat or drink anything.

Keep an eye out for birds too! Barns are good for spotting swallows and hedgerows are great for seeing robins

Date completed: Day _____ Month _____ Year _____

24. Go on a walk barefoot

You'll never want to put your shoes back on when you feel the tickly grass between your toes.

What you need:

– A towel to clean your feet with before you put your socks back on

Draw a picture of your footprints below. If your feet get muddy enough you could even make a toe print!

TOP TIP

Keep your eyes open for glass or other things that might poke you. Ouch!

Date completed: Day _____ Month _____ Year _____

25. Make a grass trumpet

Blow into a blade of grass and start up the band.

What you need:

- A clean, wide blade of grass
- A big breath
- 2 hands

Are there any other things from nature that you could use as a musical instrument?

TOP TIP

For the loudest squeak, make a hole in the grass with your fingernail and then position the grass right in between your thumbs and press your lips firmly together before you blow.

Stick your grass trumpet here:

Date completed: Day _____ Month _____ Year _____

26. Hunt for fossils and bones

There aren't many dinosaur bones around these days but you never know what other treasure you might find if you dig around.

What you need:

– A bucket and spade
– A grown-up to go searching with you

Draw a picture of the creature you think your bones or fossils might have come from:

TOP TIP

Dogs are known for burying their bones and anything else that they can lay their paws on. When you're digging around, make sure you're not digging up what a dog has left behind.

**Make sure you know
The Fossil Code:**

1. Stay away from cliffs
2. Don't hammer or dig in cliffs
3. Keep away from cliff edges
4. Always go collecting when the tide is going out
5. Be aware of weather conditions
6. You can collect things which have been naturally unearthed or washed up, but don't dig up stuff where it was originally buried
7. Take a grown-up with you

Date completed: Day _____ Month _____ Year _____

27. Go star gazing

If you're lucky you might be able to make a wish on a shooting star!

What you need:

- A clear night with few clouds
- A place with no street lights
- A grown-up to go with you to star gaze

If you could name a star, what would you call it?

TOP TIP

Orion's Belt is one of the easiest constellations to spot and is in the night sky during the winter months. Just look for 3 bright stars in a straight line.

What other constellations did you see? Draw the brightest one here:

Date completed: Day _____ Month _____ Year _____

28. Climb a huge hill

Go to the top and touch the sky.

What you need:

- A huge hill
- A footpath to take you to the top
- Trainers or boots – leave your flip-flops behind

Stick in a photo of the view from the top of the hill or draw what you saw:

TOP TIP

If the hill is really huge, walking up might seem like hard work at times, but don't forget there's nothing better than a sing-song to keep spirits up. And remember, stay away from drops and edges.

Date completed: Day _____ Month _____ Year _____

29. Explore a cave

Don't forget your torch – you're going to need it!

What you need:

- Trainers or shoes that will grip as caves can be slippery
- A torch so you can see
- An adult to explore with you. Even experts never enter a cave alone

Close your eyes and see if you can draw a picture of yourself without looking – just like you're in a dark, dark cave:

TOP TIP

Have fun but do be careful not to disturb any wildlife living in the cave.

Special species live in caves, such as cave spiders and glow-in-the-dark mosses

Date completed: Day _____ Month _____ Year _____

30. Hold a scary beast

It might be scary at the time but think how brave you'll feel after.

What you need:

- A scary animal, perhaps
  a scurrying spider, a slimy slug
  or a big beetle (avoid things
  that may sting or bite)

Draw the scariest beast you can
think of:

TOP TIP

They may look tough, but
make sure you handle your
scary beast with care.

What scary beast did
you hold? Write it here:

Date completed: Day _____ Month _____ Year _____

'If you go pond-dipping you can find little animals like newts'

Recommended by Emma, aged 8